The Crystal Sea

Bobbi Sinha-Morey

The Crystal Sea, Copyright © 2023 by Bobbi Sinha-Morey

All rights reserved. No part of this book may be reproduced or transmitted in any form or by any means, electronic or mechanical, including photocopying, recording, or by any information storage and retrieval system, without permission in writing from the publisher.

Reprints:
"Bridge of Scarlet Leaves" previously published in the book *The Violet Hours,* 2019.
"Trail of Lilies," *The Violet Hours,* Sept. 2019.
"Bohemian Heart," *Tuesday Magazine,* Spring 2020.
"My Heart Aflutter," *Trouvaille Review,* Oct. 2021.
"My Heart Left Ajar," *Poetry Pacific,* Sept. 2021.
"The Art of Seeing," "Eyes of the Painter," *Ink Poetry,* Sept. 2021.
"A Pearl Glow in My Heart" & "A Shy Plea," *Fireflies' Light,* Fall 2021.
"I Listen to the Wrens," "An Aurora in My Heart," "Time is a Jewel," *Reapparition Journal,* Fall 2021.
"Time's Worn Garden," *Halcyon Days,* Issue 27, 2022.
"In The Eyes of a Survivor," *Founder's Favourites,* Issue 20, Sept. 2022.
"The Hum of Silence," "Stitching Our Memories Together," "Azalea View," *Academy of the Heart and Mind,* September 13, 2022.
"Broken Lullaby" & "Glass Doorknob," *Door is a Jar Magazine,* Fall 2022.
"Sanctuary of Fireflies," *Poetica Anthology #7,* August 2022.
"No Bird Ever Flew Here," *Fresh Words-- An International Literary Magazine,* August 2022.
"Pearls of Ice," appeared in *Brief Wilderness,* July 2022.
"Crippled Grammar of the Heart," *The Nightingale Poetry Review,* July 2022.
"Sifting The Dust," *Daily Featured Poetry,* June 2022.
"A Gold Rose," "A Leaf From Heaven," and "Fabric of Solitude," *Across the Margin,* May 2022.
"Cobweb," *Topical Poetry,* May 2022.
"Joyous," "My Love Has Been Renewed," and "The Sound of Peace," *Agape Review,* April 2022.
"The One Percent," "Daybreak," "Glass Shell" appeared in *The MockingOwl Roost Magazine ,* 2022
"No Grave Finger or Ill Wind," *Jimson Weed ,* 2022
"A Silent Joy" & "The Last Few Notes," *Spirit Fire Review ,* 2022
"Glass Doorknob" & "Broken Lullaby," *Door is Ajar ,* 2022
"Time's Woven Garden," *Halcyon Days ,* 2022
"Untie The Rainbow" & "In The Eyes of a Survivor," *Founder's Favorites ,* 2022

Cover and interior book design: Cyrusfiction Productions

ISBN-13: 978-1-957121-45-1
Published by WHP, 2023
United States of America

Dedicated to my loving husband Joe.

Nestled Like a Robin's Eggs

If morning ever comes, the tip
   of dawn beginning to turn to dust,
I'll follow behind you, the two of
us nestled like a robin's eggs
before the day whispers outside
the window where the first lilacs
used to linger, and we're alone
with the miracles that have lasted
all our lives; an envelope with
a note inside from God saying
this is a final farewell now that
this is the last day of our lives,
a silence that we are wrapped
inside a peaceful spread comforting
us, our eyes closed for the very last
time, your hand and mind folded
together while we lay in the unmade
bed, our unspoken thoughts so closely
pressed together. Now our dreams
are leading us towards a different
world, an afterlife where our hearts
are fastened together so brightly.

A Silent Joy

A never-ending peaceful light was at the end of the road and I lapped it up like oxygen heaven had given me, a silent joy that rose in my heart replacing the fear that once lived inside of me, and now here I am sampling the beauty of patience, the bone-truths of a turbulent disparate past that used to haunt me so blessedly gone, the self-assured dexterity of my hands and limbs so well intact, the quotidian of unfailing light awakening me in the late dawn, a warm pillow for my head, and the memory of soothing dreams.

Life's Wild Hymn

In the lamp's small circle of warmth, moths thumping against the screen window, tears of happiness began to warm my eyelids of where I now lived, in an upstairs room inside a boardinghouse on Natalie Lane, humming to life's wild hymn, so pleased by what I'd done for myself; no single person, not a one helped me on the path to find the perfect place in heaven for myself, here in Opal View, the best part of town, and I'd arrived here on my own two feet, faraway from my family who didn't have a clue where I could be; they must be tearing holes in the sky, stripping birds of their voices so there would be no song. They'll never know I'd be here either having earned a cushy job of my own, furnishing my simple living space, and to think I'd begun with five hundred dollars in my hand; no one can take this away from me. Life had fed me gingerly, and every night I'd sleep dreaming of daybreak. I lit my own future, my tongue curling, ready for more tasting.

A Silent Goodbye

In my silent good-bye
no words were spent, only
the memory of a minor
friend I once knew; no
honest answers between us
that might've left a sharp
edge, only heartfelt thoughts
over a lovingly handmade gift
I'd so patiently crafted with
my dexterous fingers, and
I'd imagined her joy, the airy
sound of her soft breath when
she donned the lengthy scarf
I had knitted, relieved my past
with her had so kindly come
to a close, someone I'd never
see again, and gratefully so.
No reminder of how I used
to live, no more dark corners
to shy away from, only a path
lit by a calm golden light, no
hand nor broken glass to touch
me from here on.

Summer Tears

In Lake County Native American
Indians are indigenous people living
near the lake in worn mobile homes
and houses that say poverty along
the sides of the roads that make you
think of tortilla flats, the children
cooling themselves off in the dirty
lake water on hot days while white
folks come passing by their homes
as if they were spectators, slowing
down to take a close look at Indian
kids and what they wear, noticing
in awe that even the grown-ups
wear hand-me-downs; the smallest
of the children starving for a better
life with what little hope is left in
their barely entrusting eyes. They'd
love passersby to stop and help,
maybe offer a thin wad of tens or
fives, but the cars only whizz on
by; any signs of begging or artifice
are met with the mother's reproving
eye. The youngest child sews hidden
coins with dexterity inside her ragged
doll's chest; her older brother sells
lizards and field mice to white boys,
saving up every dollar. Time melts
for them as each day wanes and
the earth is always so still under
their feet, summer tears glistening
on their red brown skin that never
dry under the sun.

Vinegar Girl

She grew up with the taste of vinegar inside her mouth, the sky above her a pale ceramic sun, and she lived with a bedroom crammed all the way up to the top with everything she'd hoarded over the years, a mental illness she lived with while her children watched how skinny and wiry she'd become as if someone had shaken a psychedelic drug inside of her while she taught her son and daughter the art of stealth, hateful of anyone who had a silver spoon in their mouth. Maps of premeditation and malice scored inside the lace of her bones, she ruling the house and everyone else who lived in it with her whole set of underhanded dynamics led by a poisonous light. The ones who knew her true nature shun her in cotton-mouthed silence, and telling lies about distant relatives was catnip to her. She lived in her darkened hole, left behind in a hush of anger by those who knew her. The world she's painted drops into her its dull black coins.

A Quiet Manna

In my journey to find peace
a hope inside of me not much
more than a speck grew a little
everyday; and led only by
the conviction of my heart
my soul breathed open and
I filled it with intricate, fragile
thoughts as if it were a jar.
Shaping my future, my
home a heavenly stillness,
no flickering of any dark
light, I held on to what
I had – a patchwork life,
and I added all the varieties
of sunscapes to it each day;
the center of a lotus,
the infinity of life, all of it
was there for me to see;
time measured by the seasons.
I wanted to wrap nature's
beauty all around me, let
it waken me to its earthly
beginnings, the sweetness
of its atmosphere. In my space
I gaze up at the cloudless sky,
and when the unseen god
closes His eyes for the night
it gives me a quiet manna
I can sleep by.

Ending Like a Borrowed Dream

Two hours before midnight I'd reserved a seat for an early morning flight, knowing I couldn't stay any longer as nice as those country hicks could be, and I'd grown to know them so well – the nights we'd confide to each other, the dreams each of us had that often went unfulfilled; their made up game of skump which was the funniest thing on earth, and even though I'd grown to love them over the last few months nothing ever got done and my husband from two states away wanted me home, him growing so angry it hurt deep inside. By five a.m. I'd heard a few sleepy-sounding birds chirp in the trees and I'd given my friend's dog which smelled like a well-worn sweater my first good-bye then my second one to Rue who was going to be so hard to face. I'd given her a sideways hug that barely sufficed, our last moment between each other ending like a borrowed dream. A neighbor met me outside the front door to give me a lift to the airport. I didn't want to disturb the peace in so much as a whisper; and from the backseat of his car came the musty smell of old newspapers. I told myself I was doing the best thing and it felt like a stamp of self-approval. I knew all too well where my heart should be, with my husband waiting for me.

The Former Policeman

The former policeman doesn't mind ratting on his companion when he's hunting rock knowing if he used threats he'd be able to control him, the law a handy device, giving his partner leeway to sleuth for the most desired rocks so he himself can leave a marker and come back after there's been warm rain, eager for damp ground. He's a schemer at heart, rising hours before birdsong, ready to claim the barest of sunlight; he a man with two sides to him, punctuating the air with casual chatter, the two of them engaging in saucy jokes. He keeps a trained eye on his friend while he himself secretly crosses the barbed wire fence that separates private property from BLM, and he will pull tricks and tell lies to outfox any others who accompany him, just so he can find the prize rock; moving slowly, silently, by careful degrees, digging three feet, unearthing the biggest cache with his soiled hands.

The Tea Chest

In a corner of our neglected basement I'd found an old tea chest tossed away like an old pair of shoes; and, inside, what looked like useless items among an ancestor's childhood whims: buttons at the time that were precious, and a palm-sized rock pigeon a taxidermist preserved with his hands, tucked away by one of my elders who loved collecting. I stayed up nights sans electricity, creating works of art by the light of an oil lamp with my dexterous hands. Every trinket and bauble, every solitary rare object made for exhibits, window displays, trader's markets and art sales. Dolls were my favorite, making them out of antiquated clothes, leftover scraps from a spinster's hope chest. Inspiration from my such young children; and soft as a breath of morning air I'd make gifts to cosset them, and my oldest serried them. Alone in my studio with the pleasant strain of my niece's violin, at my happiest every night, the waters of my muse rushing in.

A Little Gust of Wind

After an hour I wondered how far my partner had wandered off from the car, not knowing our ways around in the forest hills of Zinc Creek. By a fallen branch a bird looked at me, its lidless eyes like polished ebony, its charcoal grey feathers camouflaged among the rocks. And, not too faraway, twigs as wiry as pipe tobacco; fresh bear scat, a wooden marker that stood in the ground, its tip attached to a red ribbon. I had a silver whistle with me to ward away bears, but too afraid to use if after having been told it may have a reverse effect. I also feared for the two of us that if we weren't out of here by four p.m. a cougar could pounce catlike into the air and snap our necks. I didn't even like it when I saw an injured bird; all of this knowing that when dusk came dangerous wildlife would come out, my patience dwindling because my mate wanted to hunt rock. For nearly three miles away I at last heard his cry and I weeped in happiness, both of us holding each other, our feelings being lightly soothed by a little gust of wind.

No Whispers of the Living

If I were to be gone from this world everything would still be the same: the morning light piercing its rays inside my window, the sibilant wind falling so silently, a visiting wren landing so easily on my windowpane, God above so tranquilly projecting His dream with no memory of me; the outdoors so still while in my periphery I've seen signs of having entered a different life; my bruised spirit having wholly healed, the years now only a memory, my physical presence on earth barely existing because others had punctured my hope – scars on my feet from walking a taut line, my impulse to give in to the darkening light where there are no whispers of the living, only an overpowering nothing.

Painted On Wallpaper

Outside the dust-filmed window, ivy leaves bobbing in the gentle wind, I thought of him again, an old codger who may move out of our lives all because my husband can hardly tolerate him when they hunt rock in the mountains; he who was supposed to be a friend but with a nasty mean streak who always wanted to have you under his thumb. I'd shelved a gift I had in store for him, unaware of his age and declining health like a spool of thread slowly unwinding. He had a kind heart, so often hidden, and I didn't want us to let him go. It was the oaken voices in the wilderness that whispered to my husband to cut the rope, the future of us knowing him painted on wallpaper, his white and grey strands of wisdom bearing his age. If he wanes in the shadows of our lives and slips away in the tightening passage of time he'll never know the sacred memories of him we've kept so secretively inside.

A Silent World

Under the rain shadow sky
when God doesn't talk to the living
a new twist on the virus is killing
the world; no more prayers left to
pull the darkness away and it felt
like everyone lived and died in
the concave interior of a death
mask on this weary earth. To think
of the numberless lifetimes crumbling
to a finish; and, in my dreams, teardrops
fall from stained glass windows, and
dark angels measure my life with their
silver crust of nightmares, the moon
always a hard-faced knuckle. I pull
my knees up to me lost in the hull
of memory, sorrow living in more
hearts than mine,and I crave the wind
outside my door, let the touch steal
away my grief before it starts all over
again.

No Fury of Wind

Ban the fireworks in the coming
golden bowl of summer so no one
will die or will have to evacuate
the cinders of their once loved
homes. I fill in the lacunae from
long ago when me and my husband
were furiously packing at 4:00 a.m.,
be ready to leave once the all-important
call came in, and we were saved by
the whiff of a prayer. I think of those
whose homes were lost, endlessly
driving, living out of their cars,
waiting months or years to recreate
what they can call home again,
dark spaces inside their hearts.
No fire; no fury of wind. Only
their rescued faith, a peaceful lull
during the long winter and when
a mild spring begins.

The Softest of Whispers

A gentle shower begun before dawn, the pond water shining like bands of satin. If I were younger I would've loved to let the sweet rain fall down on me but now I just liked watching it dance in the patio on chairs, the round table, and floor, wishing I could memorize its rhythm, a welcome beginning to an idyllic morning, a repast awaiting me of granola, yogurt, and raisins. Met with the luxury to sleep in, the warmth of sheets, the unconcealed peace and gift from heaven to have the perfect life and perfect home. Nothing to take this away from me; I could play solitaire in bed and be happy. God has cast His eyes on me, a comforting presence while the solace inside my home is wrapped in the softest of whispers.

A Flowering Peace

In the sky's curtain of light
rushing through the opening
of the trees I relish the wind
blessing me with the swirl
of its caressing hand, my hopes
tied in a bundle, my heart filled
with a flowering peace. I watch
the blissful motion of a moving
river, brush my hand through
its coolness, witness its vibrant
spirit as if it were on its way to
a much awaited tomorrow.

Yearn for the Wind

In the curve of an awakening
sun I never pass by unspoken
thoughts and jewelled threads
left over from last night's dreams
having woken so peacefully,
unveiling my emotions to
the golden aura of the world,
a sanctuary in the well of
the morning when the mirror
before me opens itself up to
my soul, and I yearn for
the wind to caress me, let my
spirit fly like the warm heavens
that touch the sky.

Petals of Stained Glass

I travel worlds to flee far away
from my memories, and I dream
forward, rushing faster than I can
breathe, petals of stained glass
melting before me in a stream,
the autumn of my years just as
bright as it is today, and I revel
in the morning light, lifted from
the blemished past, a cerulean
glow inside my heart I captured
from the sky and sun.

God's White Veil

My beeswax candle having
dwindled through the night,
I woke with white ribbons
dissolving from my dreams,
my spirit arisen by the crusting
of a December sunrise, a mild
ripple of chill in the air on my
window and the snow weighs
down the naked branches in
the winter, my hand trembling,
wanting to touch the beauty
before me, nothing that costs
a trifling sum, God's white veil
touching the earth while I witness
the birth of a violet iris, its perfectly
uncurled flames inside my window,
having woken to spicen the sweetness
of dawn.

Pond of Tranquility

I will swim in the pond of
tranquility and may the honesty
in my heart never cede; no more
crumpled dreams or fury in the air,
only a joy that dispels any grayness
I may have felt. Before me is a world
I've painted with my hands, a reality
that I own oblivious to anything else,
the tiny child inside of me raring to
move forth below a smiling dawn
that salutes the sky and memories
waiting to be born; visions of a life
free from yesterday's sins that inspire
me forward, no more alone like
a solitary tree but like a giant butterfly
just splitting out of its cocoon, testing
the morning's cool wind against its
wings.

The Sleepy Magnolias

Wakening below the sleepy magnolias I listen for their secrets I've learned they won't say to me, wisely keeping each one to themselves; secrets I once shied away from that vanished like chalk art on a rainy day. Alone with myself I now have a tickle of fascination for the future knowing I was here because I'd pursued the growing light I'd seen through a halfway open door. I paint a layer of rainbow colors on the canvas I carry with me, the voice of heaven whispering to me so deeply, hugging me so close til tomorrow's morning light, wellness spilling over inside my heart; and, in my most tranquil hours, I dream of red blossoms raining on the river water spinning around so happily under the sun, their own silent dervish.

A Lavender Sky

I folded away my memories
so they wouldn't touch me
again, locking them inside
a bottom drawer, my strictured
heart beginning to soften, at
last letting in beauty the world
is here to bring: when the awakening
dawn pierces the autumn trees,
flyways of leaves hovering in
the wind; and I'd long to idly trace
the delicate curl of a lapwing's
crest; hold a red-throat's eggs in
my hands, anything that would
put out the filament of light of
the past. I am now sealed inside
a world I've always dreamed of,
living below a lavender sky when
the late afternoon comes, and
the glow heaven brings.

Language That Had Cracked Between Us

Lying down in the backseat of my parents' car, them in the front driving me the long way home from Oceanside to the hills of Orinda, California, I was on the verge of starting my life over again, a book clasped to my chest by Alan Lakein on how to do it right, and all the recent events that spun around in my mind: the hefty bill I'd left on the laundry machine for my soon-to-be ex-husband I escaped from with my life, the lawyer I'd paid sixty dollars to for her advice, relieved that the check cleared so I wouldn't have to think about it at night; all the furniture I had hauled away into storage at the very last minute; a U-Haul unit stuffed with all my belongings. And now, before me, my chances limited like a small deck of cards, nothing to activate my hope for living, the likelihood of following any logical path dependent on patches of unbroken time. I'd wakened to an undecided river, unable to plan, only catching stretches of half an hour at a time. In ensuing months a snapdragon of a woman raged at me for dinging her car; me renting a Hertz car for getting around, the next paying for a taxi, barely having enough to make it to the other side of town; our friend George, the defrocked priest, driving me on the hottest day of summer to my family's vacation house at the lake, where it was only my father and me. Language that had cracked between us finally mended again; and, at night when I would dream a new air filled my lungs. In a recurring dream I was in a garden patio, invisible hands parting the afternoon, the breath of white blossoms filling the air in a solace of sweet peace.

Wild Iris

In the pale dusk alone with
my street smarts I told myself
truth is a landscape survivors
like me know truly well and
in the lens of the world only
an observant God sees me;
He doing nothing to help.
Me, trapped in a life that taught
me not to trust, to fend for my
own existence, and I'd found
a home for toughened kindred
spirits like me apart from life
on the streets, all of us inside
a downstairs apartment and they
were really good to me, told them
I never wanted to leave, never
wanted to return to my family
no matter how hard they'd try
to track me down, no matter
how much they missed me,
a runaway at the age of twenty
six, the only thing I ever missed
were nights with the David
Letterman show, a therapy for
the daily misery and hellish
nights my parents forced me
to live with. In a window of my
newfound domicile a wild iris
was breathing in the warm light
and the flicker of a lighthearted
hummingbird paused by a window
as if to say hello, wakening me to
this new illumined life.

Hope Is The Oxygen

Hope is the oxygen I live on
that carries me into the next
day, far away where no finger
of the past can bruise me like
dropped fruit again, no human
vagary can ever trap me under
a dark sun for years again.
I had mastered my breathing,
practiced the Art of Contrology,
tightroped my way til I knelt
under a violet dawn. No vestige
of a malignant light swept by me,
no tin-colored sky existed above
me, and never an unwanted chill
in the air. I lived in a world carved
by God's hands, stroke by His
eternal touch, my hope spilling
over, and I danced like a child
in a sacred river.

A Slender Petal

Empty birdcage sways so
silently in the garden that no
one has visited day after day
and without any water or April
rain the harebells once so vibrant
have now broken and faded. No
tiny lady to nurture the garden
I used to see, no more reason
to hide in what used to be such
a beautiful refuge. Maybe the
owner had died; I'd seen no trace
of her around, and I noticed
the way the sun hung in the thick
August air ignoring the flowers
that once grew and the doomed
Dutch Elm trees held hostage by
an ungiving hand, their lives so
bare in the ebb of gravity, just
one drop of water would stud
each joint of a branch's life.
I wish I could reach over the fence,
touch a mum's quiet lips. At night
I dream of the moon tangled in
pines, a slender petal offering all
its gold in morning light.

The Killing Kind

A missile strike in Ukraine right from the heart of the killing kind, the icy wind of Putin having dealt another fatal blow among a thousand civilians, no savior to save them, leaving air that burns when you breathe. The bible means nothing to Putin, nor do snippets of prayer; he turns an uncaring eye while those in Ukraine are killed or lay injured and die. Only a soldier from America is left half alive, lying in umber, the last of a red sunset above him dying in the sky, a sole tear from God that graces his cheek; a blessing he wasn't found by the Russians and left to die inside a gulag with his family back home and grieving. In Baja California they cry, pray for any word of him being alive; memories of him bench-pressing with his son, his wife a nurse who works inside the nearest hospital. To his wife's unrestrained tears of joy and after months of waiting, he comes back home; and, blessedly, not inside a coffin.

Just Short of Assertion

The last time I saw her at
the outdoor Umpqua Buffet
there was an indescript look
on her face and she glanced
my way, knew I had seen her,
then turned away. Before,
her expression drained with
uncertainty; between us her
eyes the first to fall out of
color, and she stood so far
away we said nothing to one
another. It had been so long
ago that I'd seen her ugly side,
her husband much nicer than
she. It was as if she had caught
herself just short of assertion
since so far back we'd come to
a much lessened awareness of
ourselves and I knew we'd just
didn't care anymore, our lives
distinctively lit yet we've
estranged ourselves from each
other, and now that I've so
wisely set myself apart from
her I am a more singular,
peaceful human soul.

Once Soft As a Prayer

I want to see the waterfall before I die where the path winds halfway up the mountain, my hopes once soft as a prayer before I knew the world will never know about me, not even a hint of my name, and days are spent with my paper-thin hope growing so bare, all thoughts of living hidden away in my heart that keeps on beating; once it curled open, like an envelope left alone in the sun. In the days that go by I live on a handful of peace, paper and pen between my fingers, my mind put to rest when evening rises with its gentle murmur. Yet in the time left for me my will to live dies in the presence of nearly every hour; and I ache for what I can't have, my name not even a memory.

Sawdust

Inside the Mexican taqueria where the locals would go we saw Tito again after months getting take-out for himself, a man in his senior years visiting his wife slowly dying inside a nursing home; he a saint compared to our obese neighbor on the right who threw out my books, could never keep her lips buttoned up, had such a wicked tongue, just as bad as the aggravating neighbor Loretta who had a smoker's pocked face, dark intentions in her eyes and she'd latched onto us, her husband Rus run out of town by a vengeful girl with long hair. We lived there in Colusa for nine years everyone called Mayberry RFD, but it was a city of nowhere; little to do, little to see. Grey skies, arctic temperatures come winter, summers over 105 degrees. And after a woman the same age as me had been killed it was never the same. I'd hid in our house, too afraid to answer the door. The only two people we knew and trusted we'd converse with through a hole in our fence. Days before we were about to move, flying insects made their way in, above and below through the cracks of our doors; hives of them outside our home.

Addressed to Heaven

A doll flattened by rubble, half of its cotton torn out of its chest after the high living complex had come tumbling down; a girl with her legs crushed, fighting to breathe; barely staying alive; to think nearly a hundred people died, onlookers having witnessed its descent just like watching the Titanic taking a nosedive in the Atlantic Ocean. Birthday cards, postcards and pictures addressed to heaven. Miniature houses, medium ones and cat condo size houses carved out of planks of wood, windows and doors in each one, spirits inside aching to reach the sky, wishing they could brush the surface of heaven. Letters, prayers, verses from the bible are written by their survivors, burnt in a funeral pyre so the dead are lifted Godspeed to their afterlives pillowed for eternity til the god they believe in reunites them with their long awaited loved ones again.

Echo of a Robin

She overlooks the canyon from her ranch house low in the hills, sending an awkward prayer to the heavens wishing she wasn't here, her hopes quelled of ever moving away. At this hour she owns her private sky she could breathe life into, imagining herself elsewhere picking Juneberries and thyme, the echo of a robin in the air. Isolated with her small family, and a tribe of unfriendly American Indians from not too far away, she longs for where she used to live amid a great opium of pines. Sitting under the hot sun with the moisture of faint grief, she thinks of her husband's mother wasting away her life confined to a wheelchair, and time's paintbrush never changes, it only stands still. Under the sky she'd love to slip away, but she hears the sounds of tomorrow, aching for her favorite drink to be overcome by pearl laden waves of relief. No sign from God, His words once so gentle and low; one by one the inner threads of her heart begin to break.

Don

After months everyone came flocking to his porch without any masks on as if it were a new world we lived in, ready to yak with Don and his wife Evie for hours on end, hear his tall tales like the one I'd heard about the young lad who'd push a cart of apples down the road, ready to throw an apple at anyone's head who made fun of him. Today Don's in his upper eighties and his rickety heart just keeps on tickin', and not a hint of a veiled past about him; he who eons ago used to be a backwoodsman, twenty years a lumberjack who by now had calloused hands and tanned, wrinkled skin. A man who made his own bullets for fear of a revolution. To him spring crawls up the side of a hill like a prayer, and in his silly moods he'd say he could count syllables in birds' songs, and whenever he'd tell a joke that so easily escaped his lips even the evergreens would hold their breath. In his rare solitary moments he steals away I'd see him reading his favorite paperback westerns, the roof of his porch protecting him from the hot sun.

Clara

In her memoirs it was 1935 and
my Great Aunt Clara, just a child,
kept paper dolls in battery boxes
to keep them dry from summer
rains and spools of thread she
used, played with them like a top.
At that time canasta was the game
to play and she'd sit around the table
watching the elders with cards in
their hands; and the time she was
with friends playing kick the can
she fell in a scrap yard, got pierced
by a nail that left a tiny hole below
her knee. She loved it when blue jays
would come dropping sunflower
seeds and she lived for the mornings,
waited for animals to grow brightly,
wanting to be washed in the light
of her highest imaginings; not giving
a whit when fawns thieved the mums.
And she loved the sound of wind in
the grass, wanting to be close to all
the ways nature intends.

Edge of Dawn

By the edge of dawn
I woke to a numb world
apart from the one I once
knew, the thought of dialysis
forever on my mind fearing
my life may come to an end,
a fate I would've never foreseen,
the day's peace closing in on
me – a handprint I imagined
left by God on my bedroom wall,
signaling I'll see my doppelganger
and be erased from everything
living, my eyelids sealed so tight,
the very last trace of me a blue
aura above my bed; and, behind
me, the beginnings of another day
I won't see, its lips whispering to
me of a young rose budding to life
without me.

Heartbeat

In a sea of snowy land
a heartbeat beneath the snow
bears lay asleep in the deep
winter and a pair of black
grouse looking like resplendent
royalty in their plumage are
dancing a pas de deux while
a tree is broken by the winter
freeze and ice envelopes
the reddest of leaves. Peace
reigns when winter turns to
spring, above a pale yellow
dusk and below the blue grey
growth of trees.

Her Shy Trust

I spoke to the child hidden so tightly away inside my heart, and I listened to her words: how she grew from a speck of light, and I blessed her quiet soul, calmed her troubled mind, watched her grow like a green stem from the soil, raise her head so dolefully to the sun before she could ever awaken to its warm touch. I rest with her so patiently, melt inside to her shy trust.

The Waters of Clear Lake

Me at sixteen dressed in a tank top
and shorts join my father in his
Sunfish, a sailboat by the dock of
our lake house and under a patient
sky we embarked on the lake; me
a witness to the peaceful man he
could be, and on the waters of Clear
Lake the soft rush of water was
parting at the prow, flowing by in
white foam on either side, the two
of us gliding swiftly with the wind
at our backs, my father showing me
how to maneuver the rudder, and by
the time we returned came the promise
of solar tea on the deck overlooking
the shore. By day's end Cajun blackened
catfish was on the grill, glass globes
lit up at night, moonlight touched only
the treetops; my mind caressed by
the hush of the starlit heavens and
I coquetted with the muse, ready to
rise the next day, hope and life born
fresh every morning.

Honey and Tea

I poured a drop of honey into a cup of jasmine tea just to see if I could steal a bird or two from my neighbor's to come visit me; he with birdhouses, painted feeders, spiral paper features. Once I saw the wind spin a handmade weather vane, redirect a bird in flight, and it perched in my garden to dip its beak down into the cup, spread its feathers in delight; I watched it in the glassy flicker of my windowpane. I never knew that it would be so easy, that a bird would have a taste for honey and tea. I saw another by the fence, its head averted at two wrens, their heads bobbing together, and I stole a minute to look my neighbor's way; no sign of life or gaiety inside his patio, just an empty space seeing neither he nor his wife were sitting there. But I noticed buds in vases, an oriole alighting upon the fence to inspect them when there was no more tea left in the cup to spare.

Ladybug On a Leaf

Warm days arrived after so long,
the hours dissolving before me;
oleander grew in the summer rain,
young leaves in the air the wind
would blow. I lived for days like
this, a sunny wonderland all around
me; sunflowers growing on my
neighbor's side of the fence, a rabbit
or two running freely down the middle
of the road, red-breasted robins in flight
eyeing our patio garden, one of them
diving down to cool itself off in our
sparkling bird fountain. I'd love to
be a ladybug on a leaf in a hive of
beauty and activity waiting for just
the right suitor to find me – a magenta
butterfly or inquisitive bee. I'd perch
on the geraniums, listen to the water
speak, breathe in the jasmine, live
in a universe I never wanted to leave.

Interpreting The Silence

In the intimacy of the dawn I tried to interpret the silence before me as I stared out of the kitchen of my parents' lake house onto the shore, at my elbow tea that had no longer turned cold. Me and my husband packing boxes and bags filled with shoes, clothes for the hospice; clocks, mirrors, mementos, and souvenirs my parents had held onto; the blanket of unreality lifted from me that it was like trying to revive a dead dream just so we could be selling it to someone new. The piano that never made a sound, the deck that still needed to be washed down. The classical music my father once played still vibrates in my ears; the concerts, the symphonies shedding their deafening keys. My father's clear punctuation marks when he spoke so perfectly coordinated for a a tete-a-tete. Time was like tissue and I could feel their genes inside of me to this day, memories of the years spent here now so neatly tucked away. Like a spider sending out filaments I want to taste the future life I could lead.

Stained Glass Silences

Like the first breath on
a January morning powdered
with light it was gift enough
to quiet the mind and I could
hear the day sigh softly as four
layers of lace; it opened my
heart like the whisper of a nun,
the braided spaces of insistent
air I'd hold so dearly inside my
lungs, stained glass silences
I cherished every time I looked
in time's polished mirror, a breeze
on the other side that had driven
any grain of sadness away. This
very second the canary outdoors
was happily pecking away at
the bird feeder not seeing me and
I'd wished I could catch it in my
hands before it would ever fly
away to the heavens.

A Fluster of Cherry Blossoms

I saw the flight of a blue scrubjay
as it flew away, having been perched
on our fence as if it had been curiously
studying human life across the way:
the movements of our neighbor Terry,
and one of the two women behind us
who had just moved in, so close to
us we could start a conversation.
In the late hours of the day I loved
sneaking past them just to be admiring
what grew in our patio garden: impatiens,
petunias that attracted the fancy of birds,
and I lived for those quiet moments
sitting there so undisturbed; the fluster
of cherry blossoms telling their story,
a cat in a window so watchful, its head
being lovingly stroked by a lady's soft
hand.

The One Percent

On days when the creek silently runs, I sit alone on one of the benches meant for lovers and loners who have no one like myself. The shape of time stopped my other half and now as the years go by, I hope God blesses his kind soul while my heart summons me to live on; me, a woman who has just turned sixty-one, who used to bloom like a cherry, and now there is no one left for me. I watch birds fly gingerly from branch to branch as I humbly live inside my mobile home, a vacant space inside of me wishing the long sunlight would care to bring someone new into my life. I thought no one could ever replace him, my will to go on without him so badly broken.

No one could match what I loved about him, and I vowed I could never replace him or his memory with someone else. Yet, what if the rare man were out there? Who had all the same qualities? It would be a one percent chance and I grimly knew there was no possibility. Yesterday morning someone surprised me; it was a slip of a birthday card with a man's handwritten message that left me shaken and giddy. The deer lifted their antlers and idly watched me. Here, where no suitor ever comes, where most are older than me. His words stayed in my mind, and though I had no memory of him, I was filled with the smallest of hope. When I woke up the next morning, white blossoms flew outside my window.

Daybreak

By daybreak living on hope I carry in my heart a guiding love, opening my eyes all around me, my soul set free and no one can take it away from me; no shortage of nature – it's everywhere to waken my senses, my muse coming like a rushing mountain stream, the sky to vibrate above me. And in my sleep I'd dream in patterns, pin down the sun and snowy flowers left by a slip of cloud; a paintbrush dancing across canvas like a ballerina onstage; a litter of playing cards leading the way. In my wakening hours I glimpsed a feather of a redbird stolen from the woods and, before I could capture my breath I witnessed the giver of life brush a warm wind across the joyous earth.

Glass Shell

I've never unhinged the door
to invite in the light of reason,
always incurious, cemented in
my own world unless someone
comes, absorbed in the waves
of my own heartbeat with
nothing to trouble me inside
my glass shell as long as I have
my art to lose myself in, the age
of geraniums all around me,
comfort wrapping me like a quilt;
the daytime so quiet, the beauty
of red blossoms, the scent of
them outdoors and in my home.
My idyllic life a pleasant fool's
paradise, nothing to shatter my
mind unless my glass ceiling
should ever crack – a dark wind
spilling in, and I let out ragged,
broken sighs.

Heart of Silence

In the heart of silence lit only by the evening sun I found traces of hope in the sky and in the petals of an opening orchid; it awakened the bell inside of me, and the language of my future begins with the barest curve of a smile and the first words of a prayer for peace. My quiet spirit rejoices in the memories that I've kept, the brush of wind past my fingertips. I live on miracles I've never missed and unseen gifts.

A Calming Sky

In a few more days there will be a door larger than the smaller one that I'd been through, and I half hope I will be flung out into a brighter world instead of being trapped below an upended teacup with only a bare taper of light. I hear a whisper that the other side is like catching the wind when it ruffles the surface of a lake, and I know it will alter the map of who I am. Maybe I will breathe in the scent of magnolia, carry with me extra patience, imagine a plum sofa just beyond this new door. I moved quietly at first as my breath quivered in the air, and soon I found myself trembling in a new warm light, my fingers sensitive to a low wind's touch, and I cherished what lay before me, a joy I never knew and a kind hand leading the way to a life I'd always wished for where butterflies would pass me by and a calming sky soothed me like lavender, the welcome air around me lasting forever.

The Echo of Morning

In the echo of morning
fragile as air I take the path
to Rogue River, rain never
veiling the sun, and I watch
with eyes like open doors
the rushing water like shining
white lace, my late thoughts
seduced by nature; the scent
of antique roses I'd love to
take home with me, have their
petals so patiently dried, and
I gaze into the sky where the lost
feather of a sparrow trembles in
the wind's restless rhythm, a tiny
gift you can hold in your hands,
and I'd love to press that sparrow
close to me, a scrap of warm life
under my chin.

Flame-Edged Arc of Dawn

I'd like to send a sparrow
your way to tap its beak on your
bedroom window, waken you
by the flame-edged arc of dawn;
you surrounded by pale coral
walls, the infinitely gentle morning
weaving its sunlight in your hair.
These past three days I've been
hoping to hear from you on your
i phone or in my e-mail, wait for
words to come from you, and
I picture your faithful smile.
I remember your simple repose,
your delicate cat pressed to your
cheek, the times we were
together before the years swept
us apart. Everyday now the dusk
rolls inward, and I miss you like
I do the sweetness of a tangerine.
For now until I do hear word from
you there's been an empty space
in my daily life and I wear my
aloneness like an exercise in
patience, hurrying my breath
on months that pass so quickly,
your innermost thoughts be
relayed to me.

Joyous

Heaven is tossing me secrets,
a waterfall of them, and I look
into the patterns of my soul,
the lightness of my being, a fresh
beginning; I hold it close to me
like I do the path of the sun and
most hoped for miracles. My
spirit has never been so still as
it is now, and lives in the eternal
lulls and waves of time. My hands
smooth as young leaves, I am
joyous as the embrace of the dawn
or the first leap of a fawn.

My Love Has Been Renewed

Sheltered by the world above me and memories that still enfold me my love has been renewed, and thoughts that made me feel like a stray cloud that may linger or die in the sky have passed me by. Dreams now carry me through the night; stars shine in the silent heavens like crushed jewels. I am met by golden skies come the morning, a robin in its flight caressed by the wind, and I whisper to it so shyly *please carry me in your wings*.

The Sound of Peace

From where I am a pale
   sunset is barely seen through
the trees and an isle apart
from the coast is its own arch
of land; the scents of the sea
so inviting I take my small craft
of a boat out on the water, and for
each hour I have I explore what's
there before me: the sunlight's
reflection on a rainbow rock,
a stone angel garnered in violets,
rings of them all around her,
and as I draw halfway near
the lonely isle I hear no echoes
of terns, no wind anywhere to
tip my boat over, and I reflect
on dreams my heart grows by.
Me, the pilot of time before me,
and the patience learned to make
my time last; the sound of peace
I revel in that inhabits the day,
and my stay on such a small
island lit only by God's restful
light.

A Whisper of Fate

Led by a whisper of fate I missed what I thought was the very last train; even the ghosts of the newly deceased have flown to the heavens and I run for miles on foot, prayers sifting through my empty hands, and all I carry is an overnight bag over my shoulders, my shoes getting torn on the rubble as if I were in another dimension like Hades, the stentorian voices of bombs splitting the earth. I barely escape on a busload of people passing through looking for survivors; women clutching children, the smallest ones crying because their fathers forced to fight in the war have just died. A torn stuffed animal without its legs comes to a stop at my feet. How much impunity can the enemy have, sanctions only a slap on the hand? I won't stop breathing as long as I'm with my own kind, too afraid to even nap, dying of thirst, and it's been two days since I've had a slice of cheese and piece of bread. I fall asleep when at last I couldn't keep my eyes open anymore, and in my dreams baby vultures appeared on my path, spiders and rabid mice; and for a long minute, a voice inside of me asked if I'd ever make it to freedom.

Kyiv

On the day I turn sixty this is where I am: in a building under grey skies, no passage out of here on a bus or in the Train of Hope; my children buried in a mass grave – the oldest one fourteen, still alive, sheltering with me and the few others in the cold. No songs of prayer from the mouths of angels, no chance future might grow, and without any heat where we are I shake so fiercely, not even the patch blanket around my shoulders can keep me from the cold. No breathing space for us survivors, no scraps of food anywhere unless they've been stolen like rationed cheese and cans of sardines. The morning light comes with a blast of bomb fire from faraway. In my dreams the dying are half on their way to heaven; no nurse, no drop of medicine to save them. Nearly all of Ukraine is gone, and inside of me, a buzzing handful of omens. With nowhere to go from here one by one I tear pages from the bible, cast them into the fire, not caring if God sees that I've given up on my faith and every hope.

A Small Token

Across the street from the cathedral
so resplendent in the arches and windows
of stained glass a poor elderly lady –
a wrinkled abuela, lay all by herself by
the window of a department store, her
grown children who'd forgotten about
her, didn't know where she could be
and when I saw her she must've been
in her nineties wearing a dun colored
dress that clung to her bony flesh,
the sky above the color of weak tea,
and she'd just opened her eyes having
awakened from her sleep. And me,
an American tourist with a busload
of others, a camera in my hands;
and I opened its lens, hoping to snap
a picture of this citizen, so decrepit
in her poverty that I'd never would've
seen. At first I thought I'd caught
a wary look in her eyes as if she were
self-conscious, fearful, didn't want
to be seen; then my husband by my
side attracted her attention, and for
a full minute it gave me time to poise
my camera, capture her full-bodied
image, an enigma embossed in
a period of time. I never thought I'd
see such a thing, a rarity I could share
with others when I'd gotten back home.
And, as I left, my husband reached in
his pocket, tossed her a peso. She closed
her eyes tightly, grasping the coin in her
curled up hand, weeping she'd been
given such a small token from heaven.

No Grave Finger or Ill Wind

I'd felt like a tiny gnat
whirring around the edges
of my confinement like
a cage time had once trapped
me in, the echoes of it of
a ragged life I once knew
that have grown silent over
the years ever since I wandered
away on my own to stitch my
life over again; no grave finger
or ill wind to graze my cheek
again, only the very last trace
of it an intimate whisper
I snipped in half – my dignity,
my self-respect left intact,
a lilt of pride left inside. Now
in a world I'd always wished
for – the ostioles in my life
that took so long to fill before
they went away, and I'd found
myself an idyllic home;
a modest, mild, unfettered
one, and outside the laze of
a brimful sun shining down
upon my little fountain.

No Rose in His Honor

They had no regard for him,
my parents who knew him best;
no one planted a rose in his honor,
and sorrow swept through me when
I'd seen him inside the hospice dying
all alone in his hospital bed. A friend
of ours for so many years, and now
I saw him. His heart like a flower bed
barely open to accept any human
kindness, his soon to be dead self.
His frightened eyes that, in the last
minutes of an hour, may never see
me nor my husband again, so helpless
as he clutched my hand as if I could
keep him earthbound, away from
the pull of death's beckoning light.
Words swollen in my throat I could
not speak, and I could see his lips
tremble. No whisper came out of
his mouth as if it were hard for him
to breathe. Me and my husband
leave to resume our daily lives and
we thought in our hearts my parents
never gave a damn about him as if
he were scraps of wastepaper.

A Lavender Pool

Past the lake of Willow Springs I made my way to the thread of a river, the cool water clear as crystal buttons below a dusty red sun, and alone I gathered myself under a tree, watched as jays collected juniper berries, letting go of everything I'd wanted to forget that swept past me, touching the tug of the years softly nudging me into the future where tears no longer wet my eyes and I can listen to the bright echo of tomorrow. I long to perfect the art of living with grace, breathing in the giving light, feeling myself grow still with patience and unbroken serenity. Nights inside my home with the sleepy gardens outside I'd dream of starlit petals in a lavender pool.

Pearls of Ice

Traces of him like the gifts he'd given me I'd longed to forget; any reminder at all I wanted to close the book on, but he might as well have pressed my heart with his thumb, preventing it from moving on; my thoughts fluttering and swirling with no place to land, wishing they'd come to an end, and I asked myself what do you say to someone who shuts you out of his head? Now, my heart an empty basin filled with nothing more than tepid air, and I suddenly find myself in a calmer world that feeds on warm scraps of light; it feels like breathing for the very first time, curious fingers of a dying breeze melting away the pearls of ice inside me, and now I can look at the glossy flicker of the rising sun on my window, revealing a new day has quietly begun.

A Golden Rose

In the bare light of my window
I watch the clouds move like
slow-expelled thoughts below
the unimpeded sun and I think
of my coffee gone dead on
the table; nearly everyone I knew
except for a handful of friends
no longer in my life, and I look
back on the years it took for me
and my husband to get here,
a blessed sanctuary of home,
and press my ear to the resonant
hush of today, faraway from
families we let go, having exited
that part of our lives – the dervish
past when our families tried to tear
our lives apart, rob us. In my mind's
eye we were the victims who barely
survived as if staying alive had been
our mission; how we wanted to stub
out the dusk, erase the sun. Nights
we'd spent haunted by their insidious
plans, the bedsheets cold, yet waking
up in our sweat, and we'd stitch our
words together, a faint change in
the skin of our hearts. We'd chosen
not to be broken having held on
so tightly, and now here we are in
a beautiful home we made for ourselves,
a river glittering like broken glass not
too far away. Living in the solace of
our home where no one can touch us
we've found an unexpected gift: a hot
trinket of a golden rose to hold close
to our lips.

A Leaf From Heaven

In the shadowy quarantine
of the day rises the smell of
medicinal bloom and a shining
lamp of iodine by my side,
a cup of weak tea; and like
fluttering birds caught in a great
wind my thoughts were untamed,
my life having been pierced by
a new covid variant, and a darkness
I couldn't name; a candle I kept
imagining swimming down to
nothingness put out by its own
wet gusts of flame, me drugged
with its own deadly perfume.
In a palm-sized mirror I see my
saddened, hollowed eyes as if death
had come too soon and I'd never
gotten the chance to breathe,
having lived out my life this far
in such a very historical month,
the nights now moonless, a dark
wind whispering that other lives
will be unlaced. When I am awake
no more, a leaf from heaven graces
my cheek.

Fabric of Solitude

In my fabric of solitude its been four months of ice and I'm lost on familiar roads since it's been years that I've never driven alone; stars in dead reflection off slick wet stones and my spirit has gone silent, so lily still. My future spills for me no more windy gems; late afternoon I've nothing left, and mornings the hours go by before I ever rise. The door to my heart begins to close, the sun hidden by the pale sky I so seldom see; and my heart had once grown so fat, well-fed with love, its plumpness I know will never come again. Now it will only be me, the blur of seasons rushing by my dreams, my single nourishment the inspirational channel on TV. I've grown used to the invisible god above who's forgotten about me.

Cobweb

On the TV I watched the cobweb in which Ukraine was dying, the earth breathing, naked with a new scar; a crust of bread whisked away by the fingers of the wind before it could ever get to the homeless child's mouth who had just lost her mother, doesn't know where to be led til an onlooker takes her to an underground shelter. All she has left are memories she'll never relive, the world she knew falling away, flowers broken in half populating her dreams, before her a passage to her own death she may have never foreseen. No clock to govern her time, and day after day she imagines a sky without any color. A ribbon stolen from her hair is now lost above ground, trampled by an army of men. She is alone with an echo of mourners inside the tunnel, she mute with fear, never knowing if she will ever see the morning of her country again.

Plandemic

Threading the light of the blue grey horizon I found myself inside a shelter surrounded by the dying – people ailing from covid and those half alive, some begging for the vaccine; the ones getting it don't last a day, and others who'd gotten the booster shot just like me were in their cots with nurses by their side. And me, my immunity system so incredibly low I could barely move without someone's help; a cup of water in my hand with a straw in it, so feverish with the chills running through me every ten minutes . This is what it was like at the end: the healthy ones, even the young dying, darkness sealing their eyes even after they'd think they'd gotten a miraculous vaccination shot; all of us inside and everyone else in the country being killed by an unknown enemy's diabolical plan. It was the survivors who believed in the conspiracy theory that knew how to stay alive. I didn't realize it til it was too late, not having the strength to move around like I used to, wishing I were at home in my own bed, feeling like cattle, hearing the cries of those who had just lost a limb, and I was reminded of Mother Teresa's Home for the Dying where the nearly dead reach out their hands to touch the living. What I had left on me I'd wrapped in an envelope and may the heavens remember me. Quickly a pretty nurse came to inspect me, her face curved into an indulgent smile, and I asked myself what was there left to trust? At her hands my spirit lightly calmed, and I longed to see the roofless sky again, once so pure and untamed. I closed my eyes, wondering if there were any god; a candle half melting by my bedside. I thought of the only one I ever loved til at last a light had whisked me away.

Golden Privacy of Silence

The nightmare gone forever,
I want to trespass into the light,
off into the fertile soil of peace,
my heart exalting with breath
and fire, let its fervor whip
through me each day of the week.
I memorize the voice of the wind,
my soul pulsing like the brightest
globe; nothing to fasten me in
place, only God's spirited essence
challenging me to move forward,
my thoughts a prolix of detail,
my gentle stillness wrapped in
the ardent rhythm of the sun,
in its golden privacy of silence.

Simple Blessings

When I awaken to the winter of my life there won't by anything left for me and it was a day of its own. In bed I lay facedown listening to my own intake of breath, living all alone with only myself to rely on to make the motion of subsisting move on, my heart crafted to examine my dreams when night comes; the syntax of loneliness and an empty life, having missed out on the passage to heaven. I bottle up the sadness that stays so fastened in place, not used to the absence of the only one I ever loved I must face. How does anyone exist in that fateful stage? Do you cope with a how-to book? Move in with a relative or woman friend? All I have is myself, too far away from the lives I've ever touched, the only reminder of the past a crystal gem a friend had once given me; I still save it to this day, and looking at it brings me back to my youthful years when I'd toss dried potpourri into drawers keeping them like simple blessings.

A Pearling Dawn

In a sliver of time I saw a card from
a dear friend and I found myself
wrapped up in the arms of a dream
where before there had been no color
in the pale sunset and I'd heard my
soul whisper to me a warning. He had
changed since last I'd seen him, torn
out of my life, no word from his lips
as if I'd never been there and he'd
always been so good to me and my
husband. Once fluent in the language
of daylight I soon longed to smash
summer to pieces, his friendship
that once felt so ripe I couldn't forget;
and in the wet months I'd stand by
the bridge all alone, raindrops choking
like dandelions on my notepaper,
and I felt so tiny as if I were lost
in the shadow of an apple, tears
of glass striking the pavement and
shattering. Prayer was an eternal tool
so barely within my reach, but I touched
it for the very last time; reason cooling
my taut senses, memories of him
unraveling like a thread of silk.
When my thoughts of him begun to ebb
I'd found his card in the mail and at night
had dreamt so peacefully, having woken
to a pearling dawn.

Glass Wings of a Butterfly
(A Dream Poem)

Shaken by the spirit inside me
running towards anywhere
all the dreams I'd once had that
have now run dry, I'd ran away,
living on bus fare and train tickets,
so afraid and alone but faraway
from my home, crossing state lines,
my parents with no clue where I am
because they'd been thrown off
the scent two or three weeks ago.
I even hopped a ride with a threesome
who were so nice to me; they talked
to me as if all of us had been friends.
There were even times I'd travel by
night so no trace of me would be seen
and I'd purchased a novel from a bus
depot to keep my mind occupied on
a five hour train ride heading east,
not knowing where I'd live til I was
satisfied. I'd bravely cut the cord
with my past, my nightmarish family
in a panic who by now were entirely
gone, fear cutting into the back of
my neck that they'd called the police
to track me down. I'd donned a coat
that made me look like a spy and at
last when I had the luxury of sleeping
in a real bed inside an inn I dreamed of
sailing on the glass wings of a butterfly.

The Crimson Sun

A trace of light falls upon
the land of Ukraine where
a forgotten child is left alone
with his private sorrows,
where God has turned His
burning eyes knowing there
is no hope for tomorrow,
the printed words of a newspaper
half burnt, half covered in dust.
The little boy, only ten years old,
left undiscovered for so long amid
the absence of any life; only dead
remains and the tears of a solitary
nun, her heart having dropped
like ripe fruit, the fate of Ukraine
struck by a dark wing. The stars
die from exhausting themselves,
the child's will to live broken in
half, in shock that his world has
been brushed by a callous hand.
Another silenced day had begun,
blinded by the growing crimson
sun.

Sifting The Dust

As the days dissolved our lives grew like sprouting weeds sifting the dust on dirt roads, our hands brought to manual labor on the farm – my brothers, sisters and me; and we were so far away from town you'll never see the outline of a lilac tree. Each morning an hour before dawn two of my brothers would be milking the cows and I'd be going down row after row turning soil, growing herbs and vegetables til my skin would brown under the sun, a backbreaking duty while my mother would spill seams of intricate half-truths from her lips equaled with her undivided devotion to converting our big barn into an antique shop. The youngest one we didn't know what to do with; she'd tear her paper dolls, watch their scraps fly away in the wind – an odd intrusion in her mind; it made me want something normal like finding a lovely bird, holding it in the cage of my hands listening to it sing. My mother taught us girls how to sew clothes, fry, cook in the kitchen, write in shorthand, practice typing and math for a practical profession. I never wished for anything, never had an idle fancy for reading, writing, art or plain making anything. One day in the winter I bought a heavy coat with my own money; owned a calico cat, the one thing I loved the most before it got loose one freezing night in the wilderness. The only time I saw it again I was asleep and there were tears of ice on its face inside my dream.

Sanctuary of Fireflies

Below the calm sky and a low wind it's just the two of us as we watch where deer will lap up the water by cottonwoods that reflect and filter the sun and we share our thoughts about our friend's paler days; a man in his senior years racked by so many physical ailments, and still he roams these fields in search of the finest agates and gems he can find; a heart that belongs to the wilderness, and it was he who found this sanctuary of fireflies where we can breathe in the air and tell our most intimate feelings, and take in the peace of nature around us. Today he's in our conversation again, imagining him in his nightly tumult of dreams – he filled with such declining health not even God could mend. We send our unspoken prayers to heaven, wishing he'll find peace inside his home before his spirit finally lets go – the sweet darkness wrapped around him, hoping he'll remember the friendship we've given him. In our silence, a cluster of lavender wildflowers between us, we wait til the ephemeral twilight is gone and we gaze at the sky's eclipsing field.

Crippled Grammar of the Heart

In his echoes of loneliness
the memory of his wife deceased
only two weeks ago is a fixture
on every wall like a mirror inside
his silent mobile home; and he,
a man in his nineties feeling like
a clock that has run down, his body
thin as a matchstick, a rusted car,
having spent a lifetime with her,
a history that sings in the lines of
his face, and the bones show through
his hands like the underside of a leaf.
His nights are spent in a fruitless
sleep; and seeing the red sweater she
used to wear, still draped over her
favorite chair, he weeps with the silent
swell of stone, learning to balance
shadows on the tip of his finger,
asking himself is this how the soul
escapes? She was genuine, never hid
behind the virtue of a veil. Every
morning he'd be met by the stillness
of windows, holding the world's
trembling inside his heart, a crow
invading his daylight defending
the wind. In his crippled grammar
of the heart he wishes if there is
a door wide enough to hold a newborn
star that she be inside of it waiting for
him in a nocturnal breeze.

Scent of Bay Leaves

The scent of bay leaves led
me to a stream where I knew
you'd see me again and like
the warmth of a candle's
flame in the well of my hands
I let my prayers breathe, my
hopes overflow that your love
would still be there. I had
found room for a new life and
in our words when we see each
other for the very first time you
say you've never seen anyone
so young. In the months that
separated us you told me of
the tremulous years you've been
through and I'd described to you
the isolation I've always lived
in; and in my dreams of a poppy
floating in the moving water
I knew given time we'd see each
other. At last here you are and
you stretch your fingertips so
intimately close to my chin.
I open myself to you, let my
heart love again.

Still Stones of Silence

He saw the ghost of one of his past wives – he saw it all right! She wore a red dress and she never turned her head so he couldn't see her face; he, a man in his twilight years, his mind still so persistent like fog off a river, and in the hushed whispers inside his home, the aureate glow of the sky gone, and the rectitude of his heart is forgotten. He, an ornery old soul whose skin is so tight it's crossed with lacy veins like a dragonfly's wings. He, a kind friend to us, me and my husband, and we see him once more where he lives alone, his daughter far away; and at the drop of a pearl my worst fear is knowing our dearest friend with a weak heart and clogged veins may soon be gone, and the thought of him in these still stones of silence makes me wonder how long he will last, and it tears at me like a wren's broken leg.

A Black Wordless Ceiling

The gentle power of peace has died in the war, so many civilians left injured and dying; they are the symbols of fragility in a world where they see only shadows, pale flat skies that darken into a black wordless ceiling; bombs that come in a torrent, smoke rising from shell fire. Lives ease into limpness and I pray for the youngest, those unhidden and lost, who will never glimpse the sun again in their shape of time, their spirits flowering in a metamorphosis into angels on their paths to heaven. I see no future for those who live in this land, the darkest eves offering only a minutiae of hope for the ones barely breathing.

Taper of Light

In the nocturnal pulse of the tide
I hear the wings of fanatical minds
that won't cease, riots that break
out not too far away in Portland
and in the east, and I fear what's
to come when the daylight breaks:
followers armed with clubs or
rocks, Molotov Cocktails or guns,
led in their growing contagion by
that boob who thinks he should've
won the election. I see dead leaves
in the wind, boughs of faith breaking
in half, a dark shade threatening to
clock my heart, and the only witness
from above who does nothing at all.
Once I'd seen a candle in a chapel
window and it lasted all night long.
Right now I cling to that taper of light
wishing it could brighten the bleakest
hour of the day or night. I squeeze
out my very last tears when I see
puffs of smoke invade the morning
sky.

Our Impure World

Listen to the cry of alarm
as the blackbird leaves the sky,
his feathers winged like eighth
notes, the last that remains in
my memory after his path has
disappeared from my eyes, and
I am left in the impure world
we all live in, time coming to rest
like dust on my windowpanes.
Months have passed by that I've
been so overdue for any sign of
joy and I unfold my shivering soul
seeing so many citizens die –
the friends closest to me gone
from this earth, diamonds spilling
through my fingers because of
covid or omicron, whether it be
biochemical warfare or the stroke
of an angry god. I let all the sweet
grief pour into my heart; only so
many tears it can hold, and the
candle count rises for the many
who are loved the most. I shrivel
inside, not knowing if I will
outlast them or die alone.

Bridge of Scarlet Leaves

The yellow fields of my memory spoke joyfully of spring and I found myself standing there once again, the fire in an opal igniting a forget-me-not sky. It was here thoughts could be spread away, snatched up by the wind, a glow having risen in my heart and bright air into which I move like fingers into gloves. A bridge of scarlet leaves had brought me here, and I revelled in the quiet beauty all around me: trillium lanterns, their golden centers pooling into healing, warm threads;
a butterfly just out of her chrysalis, snapping open her wings.

Time's Woven Garden

I want to be the flower
petal that grazes your chin,
the stem that holds me
closer to you, the center
where my love unfolds;
our hearts in the rhythm of
the wind, and together we
free our souls. I praise
the morning light, time's
woven garden for our
union, the gentle caress
of the sun as my petals
find the curve of your chin
and we live in a world of
blissful tomorrows, our
eternal Eden.

In The Eyes of a Survivor

Don't let anyone steal the glow of light in your eyes away, but make decisions like I did so carefully constructed and hidden away. I relied on my second thoughts and in my most secret heart I learned how to stay alive by tracing the right paths to take and how to think better given only a tiny drop of hope; if I hadn't I would've died long ago. Escape from the ones who make you feel less than you are, who want to shut you away from the world. To survive rely on no one but yourself and don't let the dark swallow you whole. A light is out there; you just have to find it and never let go.

Untie The Ribbon

Sunlight sneaks in through
a door like an unopened
gift and I have a yen to untie
the ribbon, blessed to live in
a calmer age than the other
one once brought before me;
the simplicity of the day
stretched before me like
a river without its end,
the wind's soft curve wrapped
around my heart and thumb,
left with the golden trace of
heaven's breath on my skin.

An Angel Told Her

She, born with the name of a bird or a river, hurriedly eats an apple hidden away so the heavens won't see; she a simple maid who helps wash the linens every Sunday in the stream. She talks to the flowers, the insects, touches the trees; God's light and His gifts to the earth make her the happiest each time she steals away. She doesn't care a fig for rations of roast beef and bread she turns into crumbs; she was a sweet soul whose talent was like gold in her hands. By the light of an oil lamp cloistered away inside her room she finds solace with her paintbrush all because her guardian angel told her to paint. She'd mix colors she'd buy from the store, grind strange ingredients with a mortar and pestle for even more paint; singing, whiling away the hours in the time she'd spend painting, unknown or not, til one day an art collector saw what she did, helped her move away with him so her work could be in a museum.

Mr. Arnold

In my sleepy country life a naturalist would come to our school, a kind bearded man much like Burl Ives who was good-natured around us kids, and my memories surged when he would take us on nature walks and half day trips, having come home from the smell of moss and ripe berries. One time, the sun low on the horizon, Chester Arnold led us on washboard roads and a quiet path to a bench in the shade; there he told us where apache tears came from, slipped me a white iris that mysteriously appeared from his thumb. He ignited the fire of curiosity in our eyes, drummed out a rhythm of more explorations to come. He took us past Owl's Bend to where a foot sized teepee stood propped up by rocks made of wooden sticks. One day in the silent spring we'd learned his gentle soul had passed away, the memory of him living on in my heart, a sweet melancholy tied up inside me the hurried dawn never erased.

Stained Glass Door

The stained glass door belonged to the only aunt I ever knew, the one who saw the world through her camera lens, and she perfected her life of living alone; she, the oldest living woman with Addison's disease, her life so delicately fastened together as a safety pin, and she lived for her friends, their chatter swirling like confetti all around her. In their gaiety a thought touched me so lightly and fleetingly as a snowflake that she was on the gentle path led by her deepest dreams. Two days before she died I talked to her for the very last time and she left with me a heartfelt beautiful heirloom that evoked the gentle path led by the dying sun in the sky, and I wished I could seal the soft glow of dusk in an envelope, place it under my head like a pillow.

A Vista of Infinity

Wearing only a bathing suit and
a cover-up, a totebag with me,
and seized with spontaneity, I left
my family on the beach to walk
a mile, not caring about the time,
walking farther and farther for as long
as I please; I even hitched a ride on
a van, told the driver to take me anywhere
just as long as it was far away from here,
the freedom I felt rising in my heart, a joy
I'd never felt before interspersed by silence
and alacrity; to think I was making a grand
departure, and especially from a no-good
family, and wherever I go they will never
find me. Taking a chance on the turn of
a solitary card my ride brought me to a city,
and I was met by cooling clouds and dusty
first impressions. A heavy wad of money in
my hands, I bought myself some clothes for
what I thought what might be a brief stay
here, plunked down cash to rent a room in
a boardinghouse, the voice of my dreams
nudging me forward into what I saw would
be my future years, and oh, the feeling of
flying away like the seeds of a dandelion!
A vista of infinity spread out before me,
a new beginning where my past couldn't
find me or touch me. I sank all my love
and energy into a new world – exhilerated,
a free bird, the thrill of peace lasting
a lifetime; I didn't even have to send
prayers to heaven to be heard.

Her Daily Manna

Waking every morning to catch the light from her kitchen window, she interacts with the wonders of nature outside her home, her daily manna slowly making a Japanese garden with her own hands; she, the mother of herbs, ripe vegetables, and flowers of every vibrant color. In her sotto voce she speaks to the earth, buries seeds in moist soil, watching them slowly rise up through the ground, so serenely birthed in the day's peaceful silence, and each day's arc is a wing, a wish hurling across the sky for more plum-rain to fatten her land when beauty falls into memory, her heart alert to the rhythm of clouds, and temperatures that collide on her skin, leaving her tanned and brown, and in one of her dreams she sits in a field full of peas eating them raw from the palm of her hand. She cuts paths that lead to streams, reserves a lawn and pool of water solely for deer; arched doorways that lead to greenhouses, and birdhouses she's so carefully crafted for winged visitors. Black-throated sparrows alit on the fence post sound their cries in the sky to converse with their kin to convene by dusk near the closest river.

Her Lilting Smile

Wedged in the cracks of a patio wall, a bare surface warmed by the sun, any passersby could have a handwritten letter for someone. I imagine leaving a prayer there for someone who may not live much longer because of the Covid who'd need love and care the most, but thoughts of my niece came fluttering back to me who won her fight against her hereditary cancer and survived ceremoniously to this day, now a young woman with an ever pleasant gentle heart and I couldn't remember the day last I saw her, time having traced the changes in our lives and the years, separated by roads I took in my quest to stay alive, always trying to capture elusive happiness. Now that I've found my silent joy under the glowing sky I've never found a way to reach her again, yet I always wore an amused smile whenever she was in my thoughts. On a morning when the pale light was growing brighter I took the path to the village and I left a letter in that empty space in the wall I'd written two days ago, a wish in my heart that God carries it in the eternal wind to wherever she is, always with her lilting smile, inside the luminous peace of her home.

Like Carefree Leaves

On a pale Sunday morning my husband urged me to save all the Xmas cards and birthday cards my friends and relatives would send. He said ten years from now you'll never forget how nice they've been; their untangled lives threading mine through the years, and the ubiquitous desire to stay in touch. His words echoed in my head as if a door had let them in, and I gingerly gave it my consideration before putting all their cards inside a decorative box. They littered my mind as the years drove by, and the leaps in time had never been shy. Like carefree leaves in a supple wind they came fluttering down from my highest shelf, an ineffable surprise for me having forgotten they had been there. Classy handwriting from some of my closest friends, stationery that gave off the faint scent of cloves for positive thoughts. It was a splendor I'd attuned myself to like a hummingbird in flight—kindhearted wishes from everywhere.

Secret Beach

My heart rose like the afternoon
when I took the trail that curved
down the hill to Secret Beach,
my favorite hideaway where I set
up my canvas and easel, my love
for art that never rinses away, and
in the quiet intimacy of the lazy
lapping of water lifting my soul
the spirit of grace is upon me while
I sit here so idly, my olive-skinned
arms and hands so nicely tanned
from the sun, my witness who sees
every change in life in such a positive
way, and the healing breeze where
I am leaving a flicker of energy inside
me, the paintbrush in my hand following
a joyous path, my passion right here
and my road to faith, a heavenly peace;
and hidden away like this I'm in
the perfect place where in my dreams
the sunset never leaves.

Sculptured by God's Hands

The blurred reflection of myself trembles in a window of the train taking me past the dreams I'd left behind, washed away by an invisible tide, tranquil thoughts now invading my mind, the scenery outside a pale sky above the coast, and a painter's gentle hand casting a swirling red glow of fireflies reminding me of the candle's flame still alive inside my heart; and now here I am, so far away from where I was once bedded in the hills, having woken to the prospect of a new life in a home by the river, the water rushing so lively as if it were sculpted by God's hands and the wind in the ash trees spoke to me saying at last you've found heaven.

Morsels of Peace

Morsels of peace have wedged themselves into my life, a dear happiness gracing my home and the future days ahead; no more broken pieces to cut me to the quick, no one no longer laughing at my naivety. Outside my window the hum of the street, the morning breeze touching my cheek; my sweet place still unadorned save for a gooseneck lamp. Outside blackbirds speak their translucent notes, and my fingers so nimble as I industriously cleaned the new place where I lived. I shook out a wrinkled damask cloth, tossed out leftover peanut butter cups I'd found in a yellowing white box, eager to grasp what lies ahead, God teasing me from above for what I've so easily gotten—a plum job and sheltered nest I can now blissfully call my own, white carnations spilling over me when I dream.

The Last Few Notes

I woke to a pale lavender
sky when the late afternoon
sun was just over, and I heard
the last few notes of a towhee
before it flew away; me, so
still on my bed after an hour's
long nap, and just in time
to hear katydids give the sky
its heartbeat. To think before
yesterday's end I'd been gazing
outdoors upon the snowy
river, yet today is another gift
from the heavens and for the first
time in many years I feel alive,
my rest I take between two deep
breaths, all alone as I choose a thin
dress light as milkweed silk, stroke
the glass petals of a carnation on
my windowsill, dream again at
night of barley, its loveliness
being shaken by the wind.

A Silent Joy

A silent joy trembles so shyly
inside my heart when I rise,
a morning star left just for me;
and, like the waters of a wild
river, I rush outdoors, let
spring's light follow me.
Today I've found the spirit
land inside of me and the wind
has set me free. Above red-tailed
hawks circle in the sky, the shape
of light trickling through their
feathered tips; and me waiting
til evening sifts through the trees,
the sun melting into a flamingo
sky.

Morning Light Silhouettes

Words are so softly said they sound like a prayer for the endless river of souls without any future, each one of them a white lily gliding upon the crystal surface of water; no arc of the moon above them, the space between breaths we don't see. A broken dream in every spirit, their once shattered lives like figures of flying glass; inside them the silent hurt of every lost home, a dusty pall; the hellfire from the Russian enemies that contaminates the skies while under the clouds in Ukraine citizens tremble and flee with scraps of their belongings, their lives as white lilies in long intimate streams; a ribbon of names that runs on and on. In the slowly breaking dawn those gentle spirits are morning light silhouettes by an empty home's solitary window.

Benign Butterflies

At last the mistral moods of my past had abated leaving behind memories sifting away not knowing where to land, no patches of time to begin an unwelcome cycle again; the present now before me, and the sky pebbly-pale with streaks of vivid blue, no more dust devils of a prior life that rose in angry swirls. I stood now in peace; my life, my spirit, my mind fully repaired in the pleats of time. No more do I think of my damaged past that broke like a candlestick; I only let the new morning in and benign butterflies that so joyously waft in the light. Time starts so far away from me but today, an aurora spinning itself in my gladdened soul, lets me find the most perfect hour of the day to envision what I could become in future years and aim for the light tower to lead me there, bring me closer to my dreams.

Island Temple

Gone. Every single person with ill intentions in my life were gone; each one of them like rotten shoelaces that give way, leaving me alone with my private soul and, midday in April, I embarked in my canoe, the sound of peace all around me, a sixth sense that came alive as I make my way round a forest. I pass by a sycamore tree's muscular arms, white spotted deer with their curious gaze, the soft sound of my gasp as an island temple loomed before me from so faraway, my heartbeat louder than drums, and I remember the first day I'd discovered the temple in the middle of such a large lake; the high ceiling with its golden edges, sunlight warming its windows. Inside I lay down my saucer of honey dark dates, slowly savor each one on my tongue, the prized serenity I so deeply felt that shined so intensely inside my heart and mind.

Bitter Tears in the Sunset

Breakable as eggshell my heart
begun to rupture at its surface,
my only compassion gone,
myself left with only half a soul,
the taper of light inside my heart
blown out by the unseen god on
a dark night, and still I live with
my undying need to want my
soulmate every morning, the years
pulling me after them, leaving me
confined inside my home, unable
to go anywhere, the dead engine
inside my car that for aeons had
never been fixed, no mechanic in
my mobile home park, no one to
ride with; my dreams of plans for
the future blurred all the time
before they evaporated by dawn.
Me with a biological age of sixty
and I ostensibly look twenty-five,
wishing there were someone like
me who would see all the things
I could be; no one to care about
me, and I'd cry bitter tears every
time in the sunset before it died.
My life here so hidden away,
my voice unheard; above me
the dampened moonlit sky.
In the daylight nothing changes
for me anymore. Before I sleep
I undress my mind, wait for my
silent dreams to sweep me back
under their tide.

Bohemian Heart

In the center of a Brazilian agate on the shelf what looked like the eye of an owl stared back at me while beside the Brazilian brown agate the crystal blue inner core of a celestine shined in a stream of yellow light on my table. My Bohemian heart fell in love each time I gazed upon the gemstones I'd so carefully dug out of the earth and my mountaineering stick lovingly carved out of live oak, the feel of it wrapped in my hand as I'd take it on my trails in the warm air of my native hills, the sun on my smoky brown skin as I'd make my way to the farthest end of a sparkling stream; and by the end of the day I'd return home, to my cabin at the edge of a knoll where I'd sleep dreaming of a river's flowing water, waken in the morning to a red tanager singing outside my window.

No Bird Ever Flew Here

It was the smallest cemetery I'd ever seen penned in by a mesh wire fence and she wasn't even properly buried, her ashes sealed inside a small metal box; she, the very first sister-in-law I'd ever known. No bird ever flew here, only a solitary red owl or a crow, no other sign of ferine life, me not willing to touch her headstone without drawing a breath when so long ago I never approved of what she did to my brother nor how she disciplined her own children, neither one of them a bad penny, but how they fought noisily. She thought she was so smart doing the right thing, never listening to what the doctors told her even when they were giving her shark fin through every stage of her cancer; she was like a bull hen shriveling from the harshest light. She was so skinny, bald and pale white the last time I saw her til only six days later she'd died. It was the first time I'd ever cried for anyone. Yet I had no idea my brother would marry again and his new wife would be my very best friend.

Racing Against The Sunset

Time is a summer wind and half the world is waiting for you here with nowhere for love to hide, only apple blossoms in the air and me collecting them wherever they fall, racing against the sunset. Half laced, half season green, oak leaves freed from their mother tree are lifted skyward and lowered in a silent ballet; and between us, memories swirl round our hearts once again with each smell of pine and tangerine.

Silvery Dawns

Days when the soft blues of
twilight slip in I lay by my
window so patiently serene
gently holding onto this intricate
space in time like I do silvery
dawns and miracles that pass my
way, dreams I keep in crystal jars
never broken but rise in air streams,
these messages I softly press to my
heart, enlivened by the pale lavender
sky in the hills, all that the rain
promises and more; the deepening
glow in the sky spilling upon
a gazebo lit up with an arc of lights,
above it a ripe plum dusky aura
veiling the sun.

Even The Stars Forget

She said she had no idea how lonely it would be without her husband who died four years ago and we'd been so surprised it was of a rare disease; even the stars forget what good friends she and her husband used to be. Now she is in her autumn year, a careworn look on her face. Even the chilly air confirmed the grey pond inside her backyard where striped fish used to be. She now sits in her favorite chair; the drapes behind her a shade of brown, and one of her two Persian cats was now gone. All she had left was her son who seldom cared to see her, and the days when she'd be outdoors behind her home she'd said she'd grown used to the stillness, and other times met with the hush in the air she'd hear the intrusion of wood-boring beetles come from the shed. It was a dark month when me and my husband came to visit her, and she'd had little to show for the life she had lead. The day she died no one had told us til the funeral inside the cemetery was all over with. Jaye who had loyally been my friend through thick and thin and now there was no way I could pay my respects to her. The only one who even knew about her passing, Pat, coldly never breathed a word about it to anyone.

Silent As Deadwood

It was the home of a kid who went to my school who had led the perfect life, had a mother who was a natural born cook; and she'd make penny soup—vegetables sliced into perfectly round coins, and once a week every Sunday she made tea cakes for everyone; his father a visionary man like a sage in the river. Richard was the kid so popular with all the rest, and in my sophomore year drama club, one of the teacher's pets. He'd won the Shaun Cassidy lookalike contest, and in a department store once sold me a green dress. None of us were that well-off, and I'd wished I could've been part of his house. Now it was empty since he'd moved; the paint peeling away, the windows nearly opaque with dust, his now prior home silent as deadwood. We watched as it was being restored all over again and it must've been several months before it was sold to someone new. Most of us who knew him remembered him as a decent guy and when I found out he passed away from alcoholism I died insde.

Saguaro

The years gone, I look back on what I might've been—a spinster to be ruled over, not allowed to pursue any kind of job, but to live alone, never having attracted anyone, my life a wasted existence. At the time I was eighteen I'd peer inside my mirror and it would forever sting. I imagined being a burden to everyone, living alone with a saguaro in the kitchen window I believed would drive away anyone; and I would've led a solitary life, my parents meting out checks for me to subsist on, my only skill making a square corner and a carefully made bed; no fatuous activity but an idle mind for jigsaw puzzles and lazy hours for paperback novels. I'd not be one to spy on my neighbors, but be more aware of my inclusive rights. A dud I may have been, and never a vice that my parents would steadfastly make sure of. Now that I have a marriageable partner and of a much older age, my curtains are always more than half drawn, and I seek the world outside my window, ready to pounce when the plump sun comes round.

Glass Doorknob

Not too long ago a month in my life unfastened itself and the glass doorknob of my heart having stuck in place. Me, left with a rag-bin of discarded memories that used to live in my daylight hours, now replaced by a memory so painful and new, wishing there were a prayer so close I could touch it with my fingertips. I remember his face: his tight, taut mouth; hurt puckering inside of me knowing I'd been erased from the inner workings of his mind and the words that would spill from his lips. I say let the old cuss walk away and let the memory of him begin to fade, let it lay buried in a mound of dust with a marker on its grave.

Broken Lullaby

Days have passed and by now
the lilacs have begun to wither
by my window, and in the antique
reflection of the pale afternoon
I thought of her again and how
long its been since last I've heard
from her, wishing she were here
to go outdoors to listen to autumn's
violins, feel the crisp air on our
skin. Now the wind speaks to
me, knowing its been months
she's forgotten about me; and in
remembrance of a past I used to
know I've kept the dried rose in
an envelope she'd given me three
Christmases ago. Her new so-called
church friends have stolen her away
from me and I haven't the will to be
mean. In my dreams I hear a broken
lullaby, a veiled sky above while
the night outside my home hides
the buried sun.

A Shy Plea

Dusk has mastered its fine
craft of tarrying in the sky,
the year's rhythm in the air,
my gaze falling upon butterflies
drifting like the most random
of thoughts and they gnawed at
a piece of my ripened memory:
trees come spring quivering that
peace felt so near, and I'd pinned
the fluttering intimacies of life
to my dreams, sent to the heavens
a shy plea. Fruit has come from
the orchard, and heavy green apples
snap from their stems sweeter than
Persian Pie. Wakening in the morning
I am met with a handful of wisdom.

A Pearl Glow in My Heart

I'd polish glass doorknobs, brass candles and copper, wipe windowsills clean of human dust, see my reflection in every unblemished mirror; no chaff in my soul, and I tell myself I'd love to be a leaf in the sky swaying in time to the wind, a pearl glow in my heart while I arc a path under the heavens.

I Listen to The Wrens

It was a miracle having arrived from the heavens, the freedom that me nor my husband will ever see her face, hear her voice on the phone or be haunted by her again, and it filled us with a peaceful joy that she'd been erased from our lives. To think that before she had been brushed away she would come with a bitter scent, poison on her tongue, her soul a tangled mess of grey shreds, and where she lived a bent path led to her door. Before the echoes of birds begin to fade I revel in the silence of my home; my heart cool, like silver, now that the one who had darkened our lives for so long is at last gone. I thread a needle to sew a dress, open my uncurtained window to breathe what the morning wind brings in. If anything is to be praised it's the heavens that make such miracles happen; and now in my blessed time I listen to the wrens, stand under a spire of pale blue larkspur. I always thought there was nothing to equal a white bud except for today. My heart, rejoicing like a fluttering butterfly in a world that instills kindliness and hope.

An Aurora in My Heart

Having shed my skin of an earlier age, my heart grown plump after a life I'd finally escaped, a secret river ran through me of the past I'd had to endure, the merest memory of it piercing me like a pin cushion. Now, at last, I've been met with a calming shade of blue, a path bordered by lilacs and the sun ripening the sky for future days ahead, and I find myself quivering so happily as if I'd been swathed in silks; courage slowly, so steadily, spreading over my mouth and face – my hope revived again, and an aurora in my heart, my own personal heaven.

Time is a Jewel

I painted a scene on my wall
I saw in last night's dream, and
in the daylight there is nothing
that escapes me: the birth of an
oriole in its nest, a scent carried
in the wind, forgotten memories
that have faded away like newsprint
in the sun, and I pause to listen to
what the wild birds say. Lost feathers
sway in their own time low in
the heavens, airborne cottonwood
seeds so puffy in their idyllic flight
I long to catch in the cage of my
hands, my heart wakening before
the hours of sunset come, a space
where there is no sound except for
the resonant timbre of crystal glass
when tapped with my thumb. I savor
the minutes that melt away, memorize
how time ripens the earth's natural
beauty while the world moves by at
an eternity's pace, and in my lens
time is a jewel you can't keep in
a box, but to hold onto it like
a friend.

The Art of Seeing

In the aroma of Madeira in a glass and the incense of tallow she finds her muse in the day's snug sunshine, painting the birth of a wren by hand, her heart trembling, coming alive, she not too far away from the white blossoms of dogwood trees, and she calls her craft the art of seeing, examining the world around her like an artist with a keen eye capturing animal life like she did the blackbird in flight, wings all aflutter eclipsing the sun, the oak and eagle as her witness. Everyday her life is opened up and with the fine strokes of her paintbrush she sparks a red flower to dance brightly, illumines the tiny movements of a butterfly climbing the window glass, sunlight glowing in its wings.

Eyes of the Painter

Elation swirls inside his heart come the half rising dawn when he undoes his tangled layers of thought and lets the life all around him spill from the tip of his paintbrush onto the canvas, a garden brimful of visual delights living inside him in the rains of November, driven by his visions and the taste of tea leaves on his tongue; every arc of color, every exquisite detail pure as the beauty of an early snow. In his eyes he steals from a childhood memory, the plumb feathers of a peacock; and a quiet healing in the inner layers of his heart calm him while he is alone for hours, the sound of a symphony on his stereo drifting in from the music room. One day he finds himself growing blind and when his eyesight is gone he longs to paint what he sees in his dreams.

My Heart Left Ajar

Motionless as a lake in January I sit all alone in the brittle iciness of midwinter; before me a silent river, my heart left ajar to breathe in the morning air while the world softly slumbers, a tree all alone bare of its leaves, and my former self has drifted miles away, a bleak future ahead of me, left with the forever toddling steps of my misty misshapen voice, the nacred tears for a life stolen away from me, a faint grief I've learned to live with day after day, here on this stone bench, and I pray God keeps me safe for the night. When my eyes wearily close and I slip into a dream I see a red flower dance, wild sage waving in the breeze.

My Heart Aflutter

God bless for tiny miracles;
the taste of bay leaves on
my tongue evoked the memory
of a childhood dream; and
me, so silent as a tree, turning
a fresh page everyday to see
if the unexpected might appear.
I couldn't still my trembling
fingers when I saw a yellow
breasted tanager so near my
bedroom window, and I read
the lines of a naturalist, tears
of inspiration between every
word. The future still remains
for me to explore the world
and do as I please, chasing
a white leaf in the air so
playfully out of my reach;
my heart aflutter given this
chance on life, the bright sun
growing even brighter, me
stealing away to sleep under
a flowering tree.

No Panacea

If I should outlive the only one I've every loved I'd be as tight as a jar of plum preserves, not willing to risk meeting anyone, my solace impervious to even the most well-meaning soul. Alone as I float about like a ghost inside my home, I never look back on the years that have led up to this. Even the morning wind is oblivious to the absence I face everyday, stupor a distant friend when I see ceramic birds in my neighbor's backyard and the feeling of depression has stemmed deep inside of me. There is no panacea for an existence like this, and like raindrops that vanish as they descend I know that someday soon I may go. Once in my heart I lived to see the joy in my dearly departed's face; now the hope I used to know is like a vapor evaporating in the air. I lay so still in an unmade bed, not caring when the silent afternoons pass me by, my spirit having given up on life, dying like a snowflake that falls on the water.

Trail of Lilies

She'd not been on this earth
no more than a day when in
the silence of her room I felt
her gentle spirit pierce my
soul; the thought of her, a tiny
but persistent sliver, pulsed
in a corner of my mind, and
my hopes that she be in heaven
repeated like a prayer. She, my
only aunt who treated me like
a mother all the time I was
growing up. She who left
a trail of lilies in the softened
lamplight and evening snow.

Lost in the Cross Fire

Alone and estranged, I listen to the echoes for safety dying inside my heart; an enemy so potent no one, no living thing will ever survive, and in my dreams I am crossing the ocean in a boat left for refugees, the face of the sun leading the way; and me, the only one in my family to still stand on the earth, damning Putin's logistics for killing our homeland, watching it be destroyed and burned. I've seen my people die—scars on their faces and skin. Ghosts blooms where soldiers fell, the young too; artillery closing in from only half a mile away, shell fire at night, and sparking the land by day, raising dust. I wish I didn't have to live at this time in history, a fate thrust on me, and I close my eyes, wait for a stroke from God to lift me away so I'm not torn apart in hell's fury like a white carnation lost in the cross fire.

The Hum of Silence

In the sweet idleness of my
home, the hum of silence all
around me, a pale scent of
wood smoke is in the breeze
outside my half open window
while I sit by the hearth,
awaiting my breakfast being
cooked over the fire when
the silence was broken by
a squirrel chattering noisily
down the bare limb of a birch
tree. I thought of the rascal
and the morning walk I always
took, gathering rose hips
plumping on a bush beside
the trail, the thin cloud cover
of the sky above me. When
it begins to snow I write
letters to my best friend in
the glow of my lamp's candle
flame with the only piece of
jewelry I ever owned, an opal
I wore on a choker round
my neck handed down by my
father, and it always reminded
me of him. In my dreams
when night cloaked me in
I'd see a snowy owl in the early
blue starlit heavens.

Stitching Our Memories Together

They lived behind us on the other side of the creek, separated from us by a tall mesh wire fence, their mobile home the same size as ours, two women living together, best friends; one with androgynous features, the other more feminine and a bit plump. The one with the tough stick figure loved to speak, her voice a loud one that could travel for miles, and me and my husband would talk to them from our backyard patio. Susan, a former police officer with smoker's breath, and Jill, a woman with pretty morning hair. Once in awhile I'd hear them bicker sweetly, and on cloudless days they'd let Susan's tiny dog Dolly roam. Today everything stood still as a summer afternoon and all felt slow as a lullaby; they were outside clustered in the inkwell of shade made by a beach umbrella and Susan was into her pastime of making drawings of animals like Dolly, gander, and herons in flight, purring a song while she let her muse flow. Their backyard scented by star jasmine, I could imagine being close friends with them, stitching our memories together.

Azalea View

Today I swap my backpack
for a bicycle, hit the sidewalks,
dirt paths, and back roads, take
the ambient route to Azalea View;
I am a free bird flying everywhere
I choose, and each day's arc is
a wing, an impulsive wish hurling
across the sky; I am yards of blue
satin, my heart forever alert to
the rhythms of the clouds, and
I pass by Virginia Woods Pond,
the crystal pureness reflecting
the early sunset and green willows
beside the creek, my heart pounding
like the pulse of some invisible
drum, my spirit so wide awake;
I take the next curve to Sycamore
Trails that lead home, split a peach
galette with my honey who'd been
waiting patiently for me.

About The Author

BOBBI SINHA-MOREY lives in Central Point, Oregon with her husband, Joe Morey, where she writes poetry in the morning and at night, always at her leisure. Her poetry has appeared in a wide variety of places such as *Plainsongs, Pirene's Fountain, The Wayfarer, Helix Magazine, Miller's Pond, The Tau, Vita Brevis, Cascadia Rising Review, Old Red Kimono*, and *Woods Reader*. Her books of poetry are available at Amazon.com and her work has been nominated for The Best of the Net Anthology in 2015, 2018, 2020 and 2021 as well as having been nominated for The Pushcart Prize in 2020. In addition, her website is located at http://bobbisinhamorey.wordpress.com.

Made in the USA
Monee, IL
11 April 2023